Nanak: the Guru

Arpana Caur

Mala Dayal

RUPA

Published by
Rupa Publications India Pvt. Ltd 2005
7/16, Ansari Road, Daryaganj
New Delhi 110002

Sales centres:
Allahabad Bengaluru Chennai
Hyderabad Jaipur Kathmandu
Kolkata Mumbai

ISBN: 978-81-291-0679-7

Second impression 2014

10 9 8 7 6 5 4 3 2

The moral right of the authors has been asserted.

Designed by Sunita Kanvinde
Typeset by Jaswinder Singh

Printed at Gopsons Papers Ltd, Noida

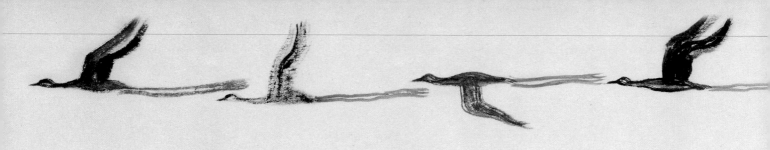

This book is dedicated with love to
Khushwant Singh

Mala & Arpana

"Come, let us go and greet Kalu Mehta and Tripta. Tripta has just given birth to a son, a brother for their five-year-old daughter, Nanaki," the villagers of Talwandi said. The baby was named Nanak, the year was 1469.

Nanak was not like other children. He did not spend his time playing. He would wander about alone, gazing at fields, trees and birds and ask himself, "Why do birds fly? Who made the sun and moon? Why do butterflies flit from flower to flower? Why is there day and night?"

The Cobra and the Shadow

"Why is Nanak always asking questions?" Kalu asked irritably one day.

"He is not like other boys," replied his wife. "I think he will become a great teacher some day. Do you know what our neighbours told me? They said that they had seen Nanak asleep on the grass with a cobra watching over him and shading him from the hot rays of the sun with its hood!"

"Rubbish!" Kalu said angrily. "You believe anything you are told."

"Not only the neighbours but even the village chieftain, Rai Bular, told me that one day when he rode to his fields at noon he saw Nanak asleep in the shade of a tree.

When returning home many hours later, he found Nanak still asleep under the same tree. The shadows of all the trees had moved with the sun except for that under which Nanak slept."

"Nanak spends his time sleeping or day-dreaming," said Kalu. "We should send him to a pundit to learn the alphabet and numerals. That should keep him occupied."

Nanak was a quick learner. A year later, his father sent him to a maulvi to learn Persian and Arabic. The maulvi was amazed at how fast Nanak learned and the questions he asked: "Why are some people rich while others go begging from door to door?"

Beautiful Nature

Nanak did not get any answers to such questions and resumed wandering about alone. He watched swans flying overhead. He admired their long slender necks and silver white feathers. He listened to the calls of koels and peacocks.

He saw the seasons change: trees burst into blossom in spring, shed their leaves and flowers in the heat of summer and sprout new leaves with the monsoon rains. He observed winter's frost and the golden mustard fields. He went to the village pond and marvelled at the lotus sparkling in the sunlight, its petals untouched by the dirty water in which it grew. At night he lay awake and gazed at the stars scattered like pearls in the dark sky. Where did all this come from? he wondered.

Undamaged Crops

At his wits' end, his father decided that Nanak should take the cattle out to graze. "Let him do something useful rather than waste his time day-dreaming," he said.

So at sunrise, Nanak took the cows to pasture. But soon he was lost in thought and the cattle strayed into a neighbour's field.

The man was furious. He complained to Nanak's father that his crops had been eaten up. When questioned, Nanak said calmly, "Go and see. Nothing has been damaged."

It is said that when they went to the neighbour's field, they found that not even a blade of grass had been touched.

The Sacred Thread

When Nanak was nine years old, the family priest was called to put the sacred thread, the *janeu*, on him.

"Why are you putting this thread around me?" Nanak asked.

"The custom of wearing the *janeu* is very old. Only the upper castes are allowed to wear it. It will make you a better person."

"But even thieves and murderers can wear this thread. And this thread can get dirty, be lost, break or be burned. Surely it is more important to be kind, tell the truth and not harm others? These make a person a better human being."

Everyone was amazed at Nanak's words. "One day Nanak will be a famous teacher," they said.

Marriage

The years went by and Nanak still spent his days wandering in the forest, marvelling at the wonders of nature.

One day his father said to his mother, "I think we should get Nanak married. His sister Nanaki is married and happy. Marriage may give Nanak a sense of responsibility." His mother agreed.

So Nanak was married to Sulakhni. She bore him two sons.

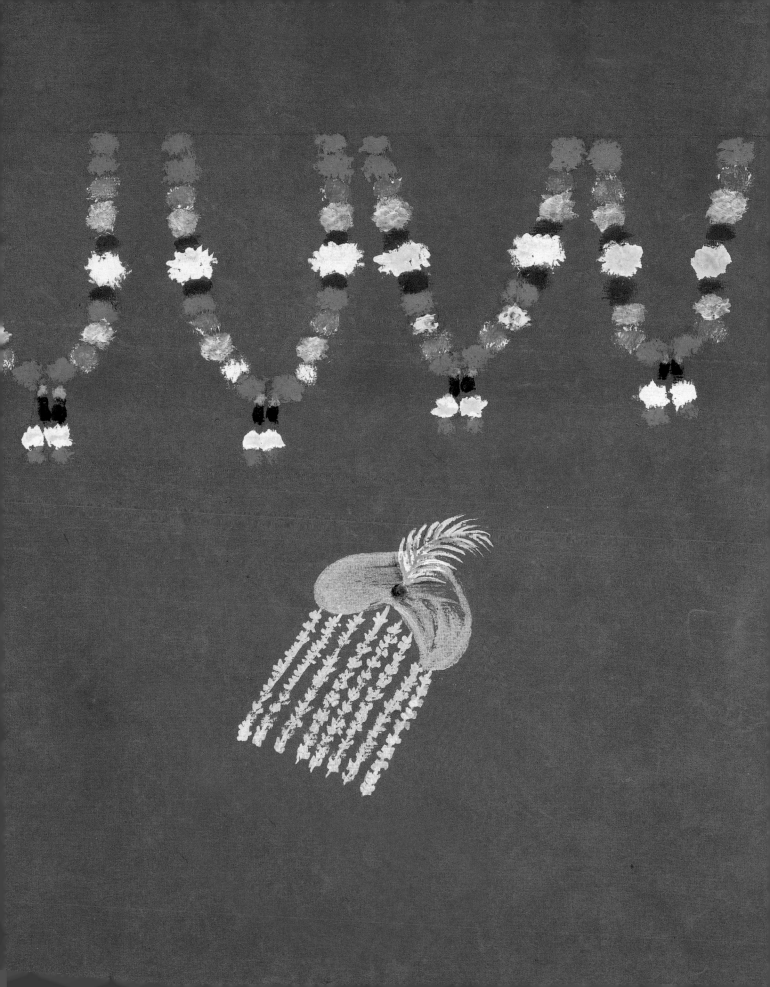

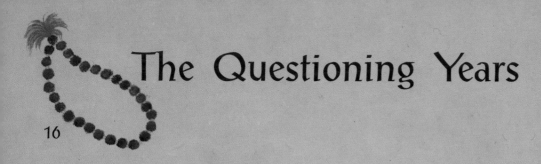

The Questioning Years

However, after a few years, Nanak grew restless. He again resumed his quest for the Truth. He sought the company of holy men and questioned them.

"Who made us ?

Where do we go when we die ?

Who made the earth and all the creatures in it ?

Why are some considered high-born and others low ?

Why is even the shadow of a sweeper considered unclean ?

Why can't Hindus and Muslims live like brothers ?

Did God not make the Brahmin and the sweeper,

the Hindu and the Muslim ?"

Nanak spent months with men considered wise and holy seeking answers to these questions.

The Best Profit

Kalu was very worried about Nanak's future. Times were bad. Rulers changed every day. Thieves and robbers held sway.

"If Nanak does not learn to fend for himself, how will he make ends meet?" Kalu thought anxiously. "He certainly is no farmer. Maybe he will be better as a tradesman. I will give him money to buy salt and spices. He can sell them at nearby towns at a profit."

Nanak set off with twenty silver coins his father had given him, determined to make a profit and please his father. On the way he met some holy men. They had not eaten for many days and were famished. Nanak's heart melted with pity. "These men need the money more than I do," he said to himself and gave them all he had.

When Nanak returned home, his father asked eagerly, "Did you make a good profit?"

When his father heard what Nanak had done with the twenty silver coins, he was furious. "I wanted you to make a good profit but you threw away the money on beggars," he said.

"They were not beggars. They were men of God," replied Nanak. "They were hungry, and for the few silver coins that I gave them I earned their blessings. What greater profit could there be?"

Kalu lost his temper. He began to beat Nanak. Nanaki, Nanak's sister, was visiting her parents. She said, "I will take Nanak home with me to Sultanpur. We will find him work there."

Storekeeper

So Nanak went to Sultanpur. Nanaki's husband found him a job as a storekeeper for the local Muslim chief.

Nanak worked hard and everyone, including his employer, was pleased with him. But thoughts of God and the beautiful things He had made were never far from Nanak's mind.

Hymns in Praise of God

He started writing hymns in praise of God and asked an old companion, a Muslim named Mardana, who played the rabab to join him. "We will sing hymns together about God and the wonderful things He has made." In one of the hymns he asks:

"Who made night and day
The days of the week, the seasons?
Who made the breezes blow, the waters flow
And the fires, the lower regions?
He who made them
Made the earth, too."

A Strict Routine

Nanak now began to follow a strict routine. He would wake up long before dawn and, after bathing in the nearby river, while the stars were still shining in the sky, and others were fast asleep, he and Mardana would sing hymns which Nanak had written. Many people, both Hindus and Muslims, men and women, rich and the poor, high-born and low-born, came to listen to them.

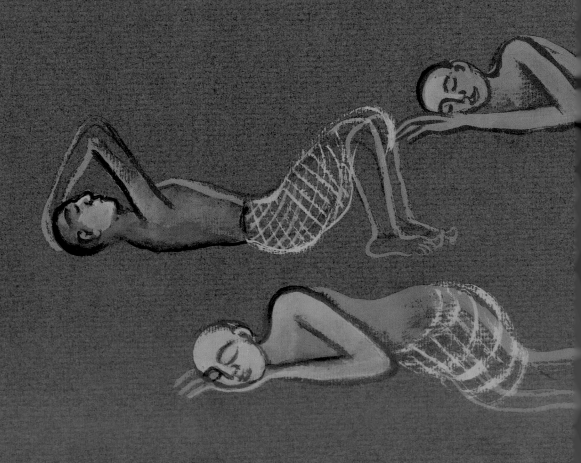

Divisions Among People

After this, Nanak would go to work and spend the day keeping his employer's accounts. In the evening, he and Mardana would again sing hymns and people assembled to hear them. After the session of hymn-singing all those who had gathered would have their evening meal together, irrespective of their religious beliefs or the castes they belonged to.

Many people questioned Nanak: "How can we eat our food with Muslims? We consider the cow sacred; Muslims kill the cow and eat it." The Muslims asked, "How can we be friends with Hindus? We consider all men as equal but Hindus say that even the shadow of a low-caste sweeper can make a high-caste Brahmin unclean. We go to a mosque, face Mecca and say our prayers. We believe in one God. Hindus go to the temple and worship many gods."

Nanak was greatly troubled by these differences which had caused a great deal of hate and bitterness.

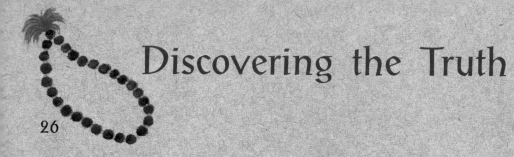

Discovering the Truth

One day, when Nanak had gone to bathe in the river, Bein, he disappeared. His clothes were found on the bank. Everyone thought he had drowned. There was great sorrow as Nanak was loved by all — Hindus and Muslims, the rich and the poor.

There was no sign of Nanak for three days and three nights. On the fourth day Nanak reappeared. The first thing he said was, "There is no Hindu, there is no Musulman."

Everyone was puzzled. Nanak explained, "Both Hindus and Muslims believe in God and worship Him. But they pray in different ways. Both Hindus and Muslims say that one should tell the truth and be kind. Their differences have led to a lot of unhappiness. Hindus and Muslims should live like brothers and love each other."

Spreading the Message

Nanak gave away all his belongings to the poor. Along with Mardana he set off to spread the Truth he had discovered. Later a Hindu, Bala, joined them. Nanak, the Muslim, Mardana, and the Hindu, Bala, went from village to village explaining Nanak's message.

Nanak wore clothes that were a mixture of those worn by both Hindu and Muslim holy men. He wore a cloth cap on his head, had a long cloak hanging down from his shoulders to his ankles, and wooden sandals on his feet. He carried a beggar's bowl, a staff and prayer mat.

People were puzzled by his strange clothes and asked, "Are you a Hindu or a Musulman?" Nanak would tell them of the one God who is the Creator, who is Truth, He is without fear and without hate. He is not born nor does He die. He loves all his creatures.

Nanak, Mardana and Bala travelled far and wide to spread the message of love and brotherhood. The first journey was eastwards.

Lalo and Malik Bhago

On his travels, a poor carpenter, Lalo, asked Nanak to stay with him. While he was staying with Lalo, a rich high-caste man, Malik Bhago, invited Nanak to a banquet he was holding. It was a grand occasion with over a hundred guests present. Nanak refused to go to it.

Malik Bhago went to see Nanak the next day. "You eat the coarse bread of a low-caste carpenter but you refused my invitation," he said. "I have, however, brought you some specially prepared delicacies from my house."

Nanak did not say a word. He took Malik Bhago's specially made bread in one hand and a piece of Lalo's in the other and squeezed them. From Lalo's bread, there poured out milk while from Malik Bhago's dripped blood.

Malik Bhago was taken aback. Nanak explained, "Lalo's bread was earned by hard, honest work. You have become rich by robbing the poor."

Malik Bhago had to admit that what Nanak had said was true. He decided to spend the rest of his life helping the poor and needy.

Rich people often tried to impress Nanak with their wealth. In answer, Nanak would pull out a needle from his pocket and ask them to return it to him in the next world. One such rich man was Dunni Chand. He asked, "How can a needle be taken to the next world?"

Nanak replied, "If you cannot take something as small as a needle to the next world, how will you take your riches with you? Money is worthless if it is not used for other people's good."

In this way Nanak persuaded many rich people, including Dunni Chand, to give away their wealth to help the poor.

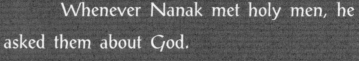

Holy Men

Whenever Nanak met holy men, he asked them about God.

People had very different ways of showing their love for God. Some lived alone in forests or caves or in the mountains, hoping to get closer to Him. Some went without food or water for days on end in the hope that punishing their bodies would help them find the truth about God. Others went about naked in the heat of the summer sun and the icy cold of winter nights or smeared their bodies with ash to prove that all they wanted in life was to get near Him. All of them claimed that they were doing this because of their love for God.

Nanak thought deeply about these different ways of showing devotion to God and decided that the holy men were wrong. "How can living like a hermit, fasting and self-torture prove love for God? These do not make people kind or truthful. To do good deeds, to help the poor and the needy, one should live among them and not alone in forests or caves," he said. He came to the conclusion that one should, "be of the world but not be worldly."

Nanak also questioned the stress on purity in the preparation of food. Hindu pandits insisted that before entering the kitchen a person must first bathe, then wash the cooking area, and scrub the cooking vessels and the vegetables meant to be eaten. Otherwise the food was unpure. "How can food be thought 'pure' when made by one who is full of sin?" he asked. "Sins cannot be washed away by washing the body or cleaning cooking vessels," he said. "Cleanliness and purity depend on what is in our hearts."

Nanak also told people that by visiting temples or mosques every day while spending the rest of their time lying and cheating, they could not possibly please God. He said, "Prayer is worthless unless you do good deeds." It was by their deeds that they would be judged. Nanak laid great emphasis on truth and truthful living. He said repeatedly, "Truth above all but above truth, truthful conduct."

The Robber Sajjan

During his travels Nanak came to the house of a man named Sajjan. Sajjan was a robber who often killed his victims after robbing them. To attract both Hindu and Muslim travellers to his house he had built both a temple and a mosque. When the travellers were asleep, he stole their money and gold and then murdered them.

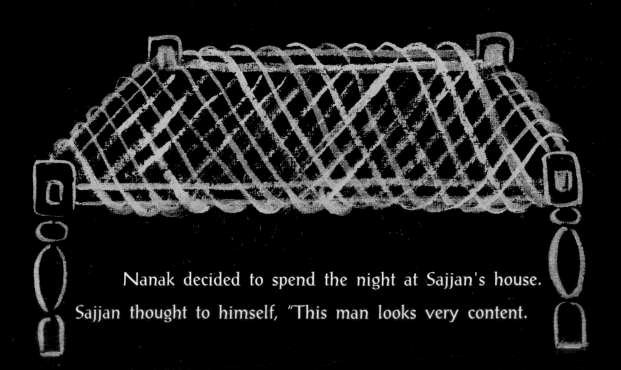

Nanak decided to spend the night at Sajjan's house. Sajjan thought to himself, "This man looks very content.

He must be very rich. I will take all he has on him
when he is asleep and then kill him."

Sajjan welcomed Nanak warmly. As the sun
set, Sajjan urged Nanak and his companions,
Mardana and Bala, to go to bed early as they
must be tired after their long journey.

Nanak said they always sang hymns before
retiring for the night. Sajjan politely sat down to
listen to their hymns. Nanak sang a hymn about how
appearances were often deceptive. He said that the heron was a beautiful
bird found in ponds near temples, but it lived on frogs and little fish.

On hearing Nanak's hymn, Sajjan felt ashamed of himself. He realised
that the words of the hymn applied to him as well. He fell at Nanak's feet and
begged forgiveness.

Nanak told Sajjan that only God could forgive sins, provided the sinner
repented for what he had done and changed his ways. Nanak told Sajjan to give
away all the money he had stolen to the poor.

Sajjan gave away all he had and became Nanak's follower. It was the
robber Sajjan who built the first Sikh temple, later called *gurdwara* or 'gateway
to the guru'.

In this way many people's lives were changed by Nanak.

At the Mosque

Nanak's travels to spread his message took him as far as Assam in the east, the Himalaya in the north and down to Sri Lanka in the south. His last journey was westwards to the holy cities of the Muslims.

One day on his way to Mecca, Nanak fell asleep in a mosque. He was angrily shaken awake by the Muslim priest, the mullah. "Have you no respect for God?" asked the furious mullah. "How dare you sleep with your feet towards Mecca which is the house of God?"

"Please forgive me," said Nanak humbly. "Turn my feet to where there is no God."

Taken aback, the mullah said, "You should always face Mecca. We even bury our dead with their faces turned towards Mecca."

"God is everywhere," Nanak said. "The Koran too says 'whichever way you turn, there is the face of Allah!'"

The mullah was left speechless.

After Mecca, Nanak went to Medina and then to Baghdad. Everywhere he met people who boasted to him about how religious they were: they prayed five times a day, fasted during Ramzan, and went on pilgrimage to Mecca.

Nanak said, "Being truthful and kind is better than a thousand fasts. Being generous to the poor will please God more than any pilgrimage or praying five times every day."

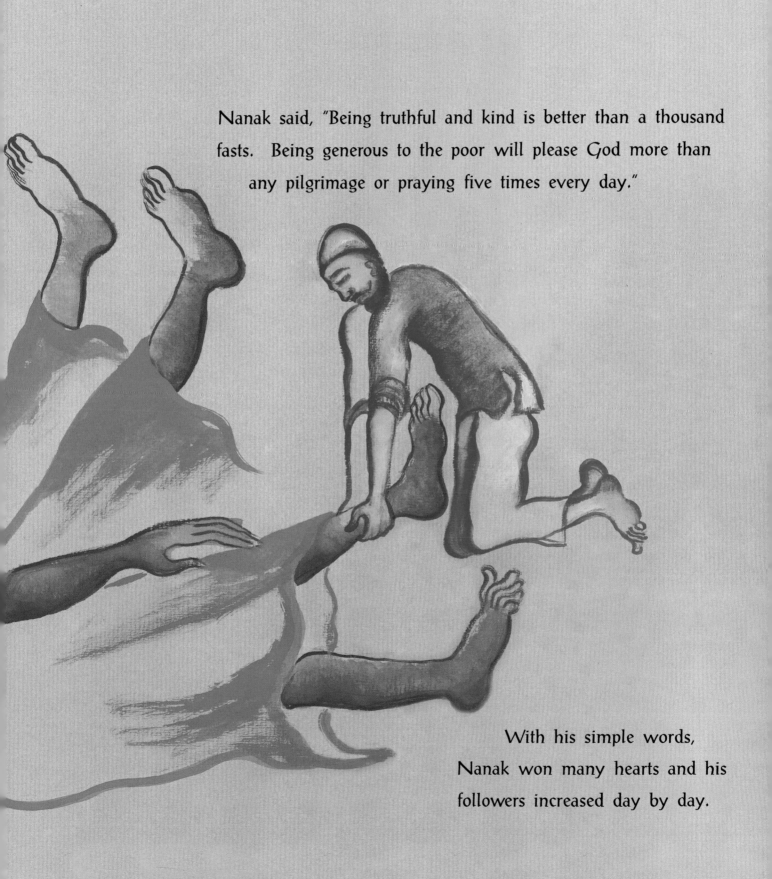

With his simple words, Nanak won many hearts and his followers increased day by day.

Panja Sahib

People often asked Nanak to perform miracles. He always replied, "I have no miracles to offer, except the name of God." There is, nevertheless, one miracle his followers attribute to him.

Once, after a day-long trek, Mardana was tired and very thirsty. There was no water anywhere in sight. On top of a nearby hill, however, there was a spring where a Muslim holy man, Baba Wali, lived. Mardana went up the hill and begged Baba Wali to give him some water as he was with Guru Nanak, a famous teacher. Baba Wali refused to give Mardana any water. He said, "Ask your teacher to quench your thirst."

Mardana went to Nanak and told him what Baba Wali had said. Nanak told Mardana to go back to Baba Wali and again ask for water.

Baba Wali again turned down Mardana's request.

Nanak then asked Mardana to pull out a small stone from the hillside. As soon as Mardana removed the stone, a spring of fresh water gushed out and Mardana drank his fill. Meanwhile, Baba Wali's spring on top of the hill began to dry up.

Furious, Baba Wali rolled a huge boulder downhill to where Nanak was sitting.

It is said that Nanak raised his hand and stopped the boulder. The impression of his palm on the boulder still exists. A gurdwara at Panja Sahib, not far from Rawalpindi (Pakistan), is named after the incident. Beneath the impression of the Guru's palm there is a limpid pool of water fed by a spring.

Babar

It was during this time that the Mughal chief Babar invaded India. His soldiers looted homes and killed innocent people by the thousands. This was in the year 1526.

The people were in despair. "This is our fate. We are suffering because of our past sins," they said helplessly. "There is nothing we can do."

Nanak comforted them. "Never give up hope," he told them. "With your own hands carve your own fate. Start afresh and build your future."

Among those taken prisoner by the Mughal army were Nanak and Mardana. Like everyone else, they were put to hard labour and ordered to grind corn. As the sun set, Nanak began to sing hymns in praise of God, as he usually did.

"The jailers are very cruel. If you stop grinding corn for even a minute, they will whip you," other prisoners warned him.

Nanak paid no attention to their words. He continued to sing. It is said that while Nanak was lost in thoughts of God, the wheel of the stone grinder continued to turn on its own.

When Babar heard of this, he ordered that Nanak be set free. But Nanak refused to leave the prison unless all the other prisoners were also set free.

"If I had known that there were such holy men here, I would never have harmed anyone," Babar said.

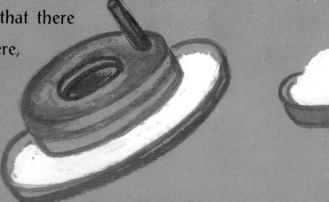

After his travels, Nanak returned to the Punjab and settled down with his family in Kartarpur. Here he and his disciples followed a strict routine. They rose well before dawn, bathed and then gathered for prayer and sang hymns in praise of God. Then they got down to work on their farms, shops or offices to earn their living. After the day's work was done, they met again, assembled for prayers and sang hymns. They took turns to cook food and wash the dishes. "Why should only high-caste Brahmins be considered fit to cook food?" Nanak asked. He insisted, "Everyone will sit together and eat the same food, men and women, the rich and the poor, the high-caste and the low, Hindus and Muslims." And added, "Before the Lord, there is no low or high degree. God is like a large lake in which many varieties of water lilies blossom."

The Position of Women

At this time the position of men and women was not equal and there were many things women were not allowed to do. Nanak said, "Why call a woman inferior when she has not only given birth to every one of us but also to kings?" And in the *Guru ka langar* (the Guru's kitchen) he started for his followers, men and women ate together. And when his disciples gathered together, women prayed and sang hymns with the men.

Nanak summed up his message in three short sentences:

Kirat karo — work

Vand chhako — share what you earn

Naam japo — repeat the name of the Lord.

Nanak also told his followers that when they were in doubt about what was right and what was wrong, they should seek the advice and guidance of a guru. The guru would show them the way to God.

Before going to sleep, Nanak and his followers said another short prayer.

This became the way of life of Nanak's disciples all over the country. They called themselves Sikhs, a word derived from the Sanskrit *shishya*, meaning disciple. The followers of Nanak are still known as Sikhs.

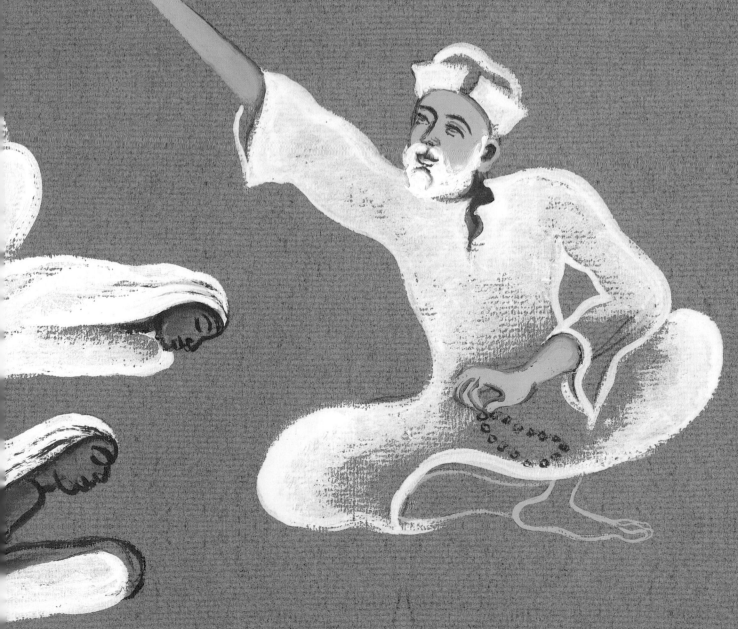

The Holyman of the Hindus and Muslims

Nanak was now quite old. He began to look around for someone suitable to spread his message after him. He believed that merit should be the only consideration in selecting his successor and did not choose either of his sons but one of his followers, Lehna. Nanak changed Lehna's name to Angad. Angad means 'part of my body'.

Nanak was almost seventy years old and his disciples realised he would not be with them for long. They were stricken with sorrow at the very thought of his leaving them. Nanak told them that all living creatures had to die one day and, instead of crying over his body when he died, they should pray.

Nanak died peacefully in 1539. His followers, both Hindus and Muslims, began to quarrel.

The Hindus said, "We will burn his body, as is our custom."

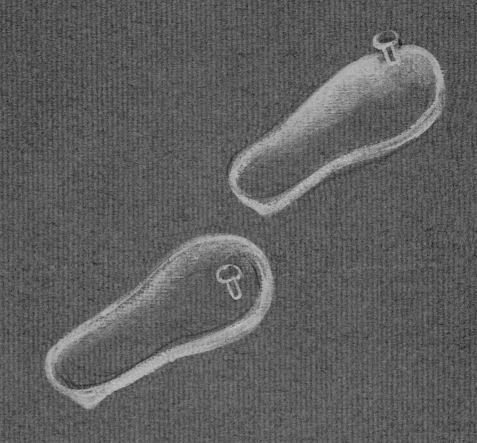

"No, we will bury him, as is ours," said the Muslims.

Finally they reached an agreement. They decided to put flowers on either side of his body, Hindus on the right side, Muslims to the left. Those whose flowers remained fresh and had not faded by the next morning would perform his last rites according to their custom.

It is said that the following morning when they uncovered his body the flowers on both his right and left sides were still fresh. Hence the saying:

Baba Nanak shah fakir

Hindu ka Guru, Musalman ka Pir

which means "Nanak the king of holy men

A teacher of Hindus, mentor of Muslims."

Today, more than five hundred years later, Nanak's message of love and brotherhood, too, is still fresh.

Bhai Gurdas, one of Nanak's closest disciples, summed up his Guru's impact thus:

"When a lion roars

Deer herds take flight.

So fled false thoughts

After Nanak lit the light

That made the world shine and glow bright."